D0551875

ABOUT THIS SERIES

VeriTalks were created to cultivate ongoing conversations seeded by live Veritas Forum events.

Each VeriTalk includes both the original talk and audience Q&A to draw you more intimately into the conversation. Discussion questions—both personal and intellectual—are incorporated into the talk to deepen your engagement with the material, ideally in the company of friends. The questions are repeated at the end of the book for easy reference.

We hope this series will catalyze your exploration of True Life.

MIRACLES

Is Belief in the Supernatural Irrational?

JOHN LENNOX

ISBN: 0615865593
ISBN-13: 978-0615865591

CONTENTS

i   **Acknowledgements**

Miracles: Is Belief in the Supernatural Irrational?

2   Origins

5   The Real Conflict: Worldviews

7   The First Confusion: Nature of Faith

12   The Second Confusion: Nature of Explanation

15   The Role of Faith in Science

22   Possibility of Miracles

26   Actuality of Miracles

Question and Answer

31   What got you interested in questions of God and science?

33   How would belief in the supernatural change the way academic work is done? And should that happen?

35   Should we look at the miraculous using scientific methods?

38   How do you approach people who don't care?

39   If I were to tell you I was resurrected from the dead, what evidence would you require to believe it?

40   Are there examples of supernatural intervention today?

44   How can we know that Christianity is right at the exclusion of others?

47   **Complete List of Questions for Discussion**

ACKNOWLEDGMENTS

This talk was originally presented at The Veritas Forum at Harvard University in 2012 under the same title.

Many thanks to the students, faculty and campus organizations who helped create this event.

MIRACLES: IS BELIEF IN THE SUPERNATURAL IRRATIONAL?

LADIES AND GENTLEMEN, I am particularly delighted to be at the University of Harvard because I studied at Emmanuel College, Cambridge. The other Cambridge. And in Emmanuel College, there is a very special room, which has been preserved for several hundred years. It was occupied by John Harvard, because your great John Harvard came from Emmanuel College. And one of the things that was my joy during my time at Cambridge was to get to know a succession of very distinguished Harvard scholars because there was—and probably still is—a system where you can spend a term or a year in Cambridge at Emmanuel and you enjoy his huge suite of rooms and a very extensive entertainment allowance.

MIRACLES

ORIGINS

I'm interested to see that the motto of your university is the word that stands behind me tonight, *Veritas*, which indicates that the founders were interested in truth.

Of course, all of us must start somewhere and I started in the small country of Northern Ireland. My parents were Christian, but they were not sectarian and they gave me the greatest gift that a parent can give to his child. They allowed me to think. Now, when I arrived in Cambridge, in my first week as a student, someone said to me, "Do you believe in God?" And they said, "Oh, sorry. I forgot. You're Irish. All you people believe in God and you fight about it."

That was a turning point in my life, because I was interested in truth. Could it be that my faith in God was simply a product of Irish genetics? And so on that day, I decided to get to know people that did not share my worldview and befriend them. And I have been doing it ever since. I have spent a lot of time in Eastern Europe in the Communist time during the Cold War and more latterly, because I speak Russian, I have spent time in Russia discussing these things in the Academies of Science.

And one of the questions that keeps cropping up is the question that you've invited me to talk about tonight: "Miracles: is belief in the supernatural irrational?" Now, there are several concepts here and the major one, of course, is the word "miracle" which comes from the Latin *miraculum:* something wondered at. Now, of course, I'm aware that there's a weaker meaning like, "It was a miracle that she passed her exams at Harvard since she never seemed to do any work." You will be mistaken if you think that is the topic I'm going to address this evening.

The *Oxford English Dictionary* describes a miracle as: "a

marvelous event occurring within human experience which cannot have been brought about by human power or by the operation of any natural agency and must therefore be ascribed to the special intervention of the deity or some supernatural being." Now, of course, if there is no such thing as a supernatural being or supernature, there is no need to discuss miracle.

So, the antecedent question that we need to discuss is first of all: Is there a supernature or is the material universe that we observe all that exists? In other words, we have to face the question of the existence of God.

Now, if you've been following the British newspapers – as I hope you do every day, of course – you will discover that Richard Dawkins is all over the front pages this week militantly proclaiming that atheism is essentially the default position. He, as the acknowledged leader of the new atheists, is determined to show that science has rendered belief in all supernatural gods impossible. His book, *The God Delusion*, is directed explicitly against the concept of the supernatural. And he wishes to use science to abolish religion.

Of course, not all atheists are as extreme as Dawkins. Jürgen Habermas, a leading German intellectual who's an atheist, regards religion as an important source for creating meaning. Indeed, he warns Europe that our educational system, our legal system, our human rights are all derivative from the Judeo-Christian tradition. And interestingly he, one of the leading intellectual atheists on the Continent, adds: "To this day, we have no other source. Everything else is postmodern chatter." That's a fascinating statement for an intellectual atheist.

I was reminded of that origin of our educational institutions as I looked up at your magnificent philosophy building. It's the only one in the world I've ever seen to bear the inscription: "What is man that you are mindful of him?" Ladies and gentlemen, students of Harvard, you stand in a tradition that at its inception saw no contradiction between the highest intellectual aspirations and belief in God, even in the philosophy department. I don't know what it's like here now. But certainly, philosophers did not believe then that belief in God was an insult to the intellect.

QUESTIONS FOR DISCUSSION

Do you have close friends, as Professor Lennox does, who do not share your worldview? How do you engage them in conversation about those worldviews?

What do you think the general climate on campus is? Is belief in God an insult to the intellect? Why?

? For an audience question related to this topic (*Could you tell us a little bit more about what got you interested in these questions of the supernatural, God and the relation to science?*), see page 31.

THE REAL CONFLICT: WORLDVIEWS

The new atheists are determined to spread the myth that science and belief in God are incompatible. I say "myth" because it's very easy to see that that is far too simplistic an analysis. How can science and belief in God be essentially incompatible when, for instance, so many leading scientists at my own University of Oxford believe in God? I can name the heads of several scientific departments, world-famous in their fields – nanotechnology, electrical engineering and so on – who are believers in God. And in this country, just to name one, William Phillips, Nobel Prize winner for physics is a believer in God.

It is clear that brilliant science can be done by atheists and brilliant science can be done by believers in God, which shows us, ladies and gentlemen, that the conflict, which is real, lies much deeper in. It is not simplistically between science and belief in God and the supernatural. It is between two worldviews, two concepts of the nature of ultimate reality: naturalism and theism.

Naturalism (or materialism – there's very little difference between them) essentially believes that this universe (or the multiverse) is all that exists. That has implications for the nature of explanation. It means that explanation, by definition, must be reductionist, that is, from the bottom up, because there is no transcendence, there is no ultimate top down causation. That was the view of the Greek Atomists, Democritus and Leucippus.

But also at that time, there were philosophers like Socrates and Plato and Aristotle and they did not accept that view. They believed there was transcendence, there was something more than the material universe.

And those two worldviews – naturalism and theism – come barreling up through history and they divide us in this room tonight and they divide the professors in the academy both in Oxford and in Cambridge, in England and in Massachusetts.

So, what we're talking about, ladies and gentlemen, is worldviews. Belief systems. The one is naturalism and the other is theism and it's just here that we encounter the first confusion.

QUESTIONS FOR DISCUSSION

How does shifting the conflict from science/religion to naturalism/theism make a difference?

Which way does your worldview tend: naturalism or theism? How would your understanding of reality be different if you adopted the opposite worldview from the one you hold?

If you find yourself an intellectual theist but practical naturalist, or vice versa, how could you align your beliefs and practice to be consistent?

THE FIRST CONFUSION: NATURE OF FAITH

When I debated Princeton professor Peter Singer in Australia recently, he started by saying that his chief objection to religious belief was that people remained in the faith in which they'd been brought up with the implication that I, with my Christian parents, was a prime example.

So, just to redress the balance, I asked him publicly about his parents. I said, "Peter, were your parents atheists?" And he said, "Yes, they were." So, I said, "You remained in the faith in which you were brought up then." "Oh but," he said, "it isn't a faith." "Really," I said, "I was under the impression you *believed* it."

Myth: Faith is a religious concept. Now, ladies and gentlemen, that little spat – and I got on very well with Peter Singer, you can watch the debate online – is very revealing because it's consistent with the attitude of the new atheists who regard faith as a religious word which, by definition, means believing where there is no evidence. In their view, atheism isn't a faith.

It is very important to see, however, that atheism is just as much a belief system as theism. The first believes that this universe is the ultimate reality. The latter believes that God is the ultimate reality. So, the burning question is: What evidence is there for the *veritas* of either of them, the truth of either of them? In particular, what way does science point?

Myth: Faith is not evidence-based. We need to be clear that the kind of faith that the new atheists are describing is what most of us would call blind faith, which we all admit is dangerous. But faith in its ordinary dictionary sense derives from the word *fides* – it means "trust" – and all of us know that we don't usually trust people unless there's evidence to do so. (We don't trust the banks either, unless there's evidence to do so, but that's another story!) The banking crisis has at least taught all of us the difference between evidence-based faith and non-evidenced-based faith.

I cannot, of course, speak for other religions. They must rightly speak for themselves. But I'd like to make it very clear that Christianity is an evidence-based faith. One of the central statements of the Gospel of John is: "These things are written that you might believe that Jesus is the Christ, the Son of God, and that believing, you might have life in his name." In other words, "Here's the evidence. I've selected it in order for it to provide a basis for your trust, for your confidence, for your faith."

I'll come back to this matter of faith later, but I now want to address the question: What way does science point? I claim that science points towards God. The atheists claim it points in the opposite direction. I want to call as witness, first of all, the history of science.

Myth: Faith and science are historical enemies. It is no accident that when Harvard was founded, belief in God was written into its motto and onto its philosophy building. Because historians of science like my former colleague at Oxford, John Hedley Brooke, usually will agree with some version of what is often called Merton's Thesis. The best formulation of it, I think, is due to C.S. Lewis who said: "Men became scientific because they expected law in nature, and they expected law in nature because they believed in a law giver." The great pioneers of science – Galileo, Kepler, Newton, Clerk Maxwell, Babbage and so on – were all believers in God.

Some years ago I had the opportunity to give the very first lecture on the topic of God and science in The University of Novosibirsk in Siberia. I was invited by the Provost of the

University to give a lecture on why a mathematician believes in God. It was the very first lecture on that topic in the university in 75 years.

When I mentioned the fact that Newton and Galileo were believers, I noticed anger rising in the front row of heavyweight professors. So, I stopped and I said, "What's the matter?" And they said, "Why were we never told this?" And I said, "Can't you guess?" They'd never been told. It was totally new to them that the founders of modern science were believers in God.

Now, you laugh but actually, we need to think carefully about the implications of that, because the one thing it demonstrates is that belief in God and supernature were not, at the beginning of modern science, incompatible with science in the slightest degree. It was exactly the opposite.

So, what has happened? Why is it that I'm even having to give a lecture on this topic at Harvard? Why isn't it that we do still believe that there's something more than the natural world if there is such a deep-seated harmony between science and belief in God?

Myth: Science is the only way to truth. There is widespread confusion about the reach of science. Alex Rosenberg in his book *The Atheist's Guide to Reality* says: "The mistake is to think that there is any more to reality than the laws of nature that science discovers." Rosenberg espouses scientism: the notion that science is the only way to truth.

Bertrand Russell summarized this viewpoint by saying, "What science cannot tell us, mankind cannot know." Now, Russell was quite a brilliant logician but his logic failed him badly when he made that statement. Think of the statement itself: "What science cannot tell us, mankind cannot know." Is it a statement of science? No. So if it is true, then it itself tells us that we cannot know it. This is what we call a logically incoherent statement. If it's true, it's false.

Far more sensible is the view of Nobel Prize winner Sir Peter Medawar who said, "It's so easy to see the limits of science. It cannot answer the questions of a child: Where am I coming from? What is the meaning of life? Where am I going to?" We need to go outside science for answers to such questions.

We need, ladies and gentlemen, to grasp that science does not define the limit of rationality. Rationality is bigger than science. Einstein, of course, saw it clearly. He said, "You can speak of the ethical foundation of science but you cannot speak of the scientific foundations of ethics." He saw that there were realms into which science cannot go.

Of course, that's obvious at Harvard, isn't it? I do believe you still have some humanities departments left, don't you? Because if science was the only way to truth, you'd have to shut those departments tomorrow. And I don't think you'd want to do that and neither would I. The very existence of the humanities shows that scientism is false.

QUESTIONS FOR DISCUSSION

Do you agree that scientism is the reigning view? Can you think of examples you've seen, heard or read recently?

If "rationality is bigger than science," as Professor Lennox argues, what are other ways to find truth?

Do you find the debunking of any of these "myths" surprising? Compelling? Questionable?

SECOND CONFUSION: NATURE OF EXPLANATION

There is also considerable confusion about the nature of explanation. It seems to me that a great deal of atheist confusion today is that their concept of God is not one that I would share for a moment. Their idea of God is a God of the gaps.

Myth: God of the gaps. In Novosibirsk, I was criticized by one of the professors. He came up to the blackboard, drew a stroke of lightening and said, "This is absurd, what we're listening to. You see, the ancients used to believe that the gods were behind thunder and lightning. And then we learned to do some atmospheric physics and we found it wasn't the gods. Exit space for God." That's the concept of the God of the gaps: "I can't explain it, therefore, God did it." A bit more science, a bit less space for God.

Now, if you believe in a God like that, it's clear that you've got to make a choice between God and science because of the way in which you have defined God: as science increases, by definition, God decreases. But what if you don't believe in a God like that? I certainly don't. My God is not a God of the gaps. He's the God of the whole show, both of the bits we don't understand and the bits we do.

When Isaac Newton discovered his law of gravitation, he didn't say, "Wonderful. I've now got a law and a mathematical description of how it works; I don't need God." He didn't do that. What he did was write the most brilliant book in the history of science, *The Principia Mathematica*, expressing the hope that it would persuade the thinking person to believe in God.

In other words, the more he understood of science, the more he admired the genius of the God who did it that way. His God was not a God of the gaps.

Myth: Mechanisms exclude agents. Steven Hawking in a

recent book (to which I've responded in my little book, *God and Steven Hawking*) says we've got to choose between God and gravity. But this is nonsense as a simple illustration will show.

If I were to have a Ford Galaxy motorcar here and said to you, "Look, I want to offer you two explanations for this car. The one is the law of internal combustion and mechanical engineering: a law-mechanism explanation. The other is Henry Ford. Please choose." You'd say, "That is absurd. You need both explanations."

Now, this is extremely important. To realize that explanation comes in different kinds. If you want a complete explanation of the Ford Galaxy, you have to have a law-mechanism explanation – the scientific one – and you have to have an agent explanation, in terms of Henry Ford.

Please notice these different kinds of explanation do not contradict each other. Yet the idea is going around, spread virulently by one of the Dawkins 'memes,' I suppose, that you must choose between them. In philosophical terms that is to commit a very elementary category mistake.

The existence – and I'm wording this very carefully – the existence of a mechanism that does something is not, in itself, an argument for the non-existence of an agent who designed that mechanism.

There is, therefore, no necessary conflict between scientific explanations of how the universe works and belief in God who created and sustains that universe. We must not assume that there's only one level of explanation.

QUESTIONS FOR DISCUSSION

Professor Lennox says that he does not believe in a "God of the gaps" but rather, "God of the whole show." In the Q&A he refers to a "God who is extremely interested in people who don't care" (see page 38). What is your view of who God is (or is not)? How did you come to this view?

THE ROLE OF FAITH IN SCIENCE

As I said earlier, it is a widespread myth that faith: A) is a purely religious concept and B) means believing where there's no evidence. Both of those definitions are wrong. I've discussed the second, now let's come to the first.

What about the role of faith in science? It is vastly important, of course. Einstein saw that every scientist has as a fundamental belief that the universe is rationally intelligible. He could not imagine a scientist without, as he put it, "that faith."

Let's think about it this way. Nobel Prizewinner Eugene Wigner wrote a wonderful paper in 1961 that is much loved of mathematicians. It is entitled, *The Unreasonable Effectiveness of Mathematics.*

The issue is this: How is it that a bright Harvard mathematician, thinking in her mind in here, comes up with equations that describe the universe out there? How does that work? Reflection on it led Einstein to say, "The only incomprehensible thing about the universe is that it's comprehensible."

Naturalism undermines the search for truth. Einstein's comment leads me to claim that one of the greatest evidences that naturalism is false is the very fact that we can do science.

It starts with something Darwin wrote. Let me read it to you: "With me, the horrid doubt always arises whether the convictions of man's mind, which has been developed from the mind of lower animals, are of any value or at all trustworthy. Would anyone trust in the convictions of a monkey's mind if there are any convictions in such a mind?"

That statement is at the moment receiving considerable attention for the following reason. Many people hold that the driving force of the natural processes that eventually produced our human cognitive faculties were not primarily concerned with truth at all but with survival. And we all know what has generally happened and still happens to truth when individuals or commercial enterprises or nations motivated by what Dawkins calls their "selfish genes" feel themselves threatened in the struggle for survival. They are essentially obliged to regard thought as some kind of neurophysiological phenomenon. And from the evolutionary perspective, the neurophysiology might, of course, be adaptive.

But why, for one moment, would one think that beliefs caused by the neurophysiology should be mostly true? After all, as the chemist J.B.S. Haldane pointed out long ago: "If the thoughts in my mind are just motions of atoms in my brain, a mechanism that has arisen by mindless, unguided processes, why should I believe anything it tells me, including the fact that it's made of atoms?"

One of America's leading philosophers, Alvin Plantinga, draws out the implications this way: "If Dawkins is right and we are the product of mindless, unguided natural processes, then he has given us strong reason to doubt the reliability of human cognitive faculties and therefore, inevitably to doubt the validity of any belief that they produce including Dawkins' own science and his atheism. His biology and his belief in naturalism would therefore appear to be at war with each other in a conflict that has nothing to do with God."

I suggest to you, therefore, ladies and gentlemen, that it's not irrational to believe in supernature. What is irrational is to believe in naturalism. The boot is entirely on the other foot.

Atheistic reductionism undermines the foundations of the very rationality needed to construct any argument of any kind, whatsoever. The new atheists have signally failed to appreciate the catastrophic implications of their view for science.

A very interesting sidelight is thrown on this by Friedrich Nietzsche. Listen to this: "Only if we assume a God" – this is Nietzsche – "only if we assume a God who is morally our like can 'truth' and the search for truth be at all something meaningful and promising of success. This God left aside, the question is permitted whether being deceived is not one of the conditions of life."

So, ladies and gentlemen, my basic argument tonight is this. We all know that we can do science. And since we can do science, I reject a naturalism that undermines the foundations of the rationality I need to do that science.

Rationality as evidence for God. On the other hand, the worldview of Biblical theism, which I espouse, is completely coherent in its explanation of why the universe is rationally intelligible. Because it teaches me that the universe out there and the mind in here are ultimately traceable to the same intelligent God. Naturalism, I submit, is incapable of explaining itself. So rational explanation has a legitimate claim to universality, but natural explanation does not.

And ironically, particularly recent science suggests that naturalism is doomed because it teaches that the universe is a causally closed system by definition. This means, of course, that everything can be explained reductionalistically in terms of physical and chemical processes. But naturalists cannot explain their own scientific theories or mathematical equations in terms of mere physical or chemical processes for the simple reason that theories, laws and equations are not physical. They are immaterial.

We live in the information age in which we have discovered that information is a fundamental quantity that is not reducible to physics and chemistry. It is not material. So, the irony of naturalism is that we're now beginning to realize the fundamental importance of something that's non-material, which therefore does not fit within a naturalistic worldview.

It's a very interesting intellectual situation to be in. I want to suggest that the very existence of rationality is an outpost, so to speak, of the image of God that opens up the conceptual space to seeing that limiting ourselves to a naturalistic explanation is destroying the possibility of all explanation together.

Semiotics as evidence for God. The immateriality of information implies that we cannot reduce information to physics and chemistry. Let me illustrate by recalling an incident. I'm a fellow of Green Templeton College in Oxford and regularly enjoy dinners with our guests. The seating arrangements are fixed in advance, so you can't adjust where you're sitting, even if you wished to. One evening, I found myself sitting beside a biochemist. He inevitably asked what I did. "I'm a pure mathematician," I said.

"Oh," he said, "how dreadfully boring."

Somewhat startled I replied, "Oh, but I try to make up for it by being interested in the big questions of life."

He said, "Like what?"

"Well," I said, "like the status of the universe, is it created or not?"

"Oh dear," he said, "it's far worse than I thought." He said, "Listen. The bottom line is this: I'm an atheist. I'm a reductionist. We're going to have an awful evening. We've nothing to talk about and that's that."

The problem was that he seemed to mean it!

"Well," I said, "you know, it's not all that bad, is it? For instance, I'm fascinated by reductionism. I know at least three kinds of reductionism. Which kind are you?"

Well, he wasn't quite sure, so I said, "I suspect like me you are a methodological reductionist. You take a big problem, split it into little problems, solve the little problems and hope that will give you insight into the big problem you started with."

"Yes," he said, "I do that."

"Good," I said. "We agree on that then, so we have something to talk about." I went on, "However, I think you're an ontological reductionist (*ontos*, Greek: being). You believe everything can be reduced to physics and chemistry."

He said, "That's right. That's my basic approach."

So, I said, "Let's do an experiment then."

He said, "What? Here at the table?"

I said, "Sure, this is Oxford." I then picked up the printed menu that was sitting on the table. It said, "Roast Chicken" and that not even in French but in English.

And he said, "What's the problem with that?"

I said, "You're a reductionist. You think everything can be explained in terms of physics and chemistry. Now, look at these marks on the paper R O A S T. But they are not just random marks. They're semiotic (*semion*, Greek: a sign). Put together that way we see that they carry meaning."

He said, "That's right, so what's the problem?"

"Okay." I said, "You explain to me the semiotic dimension of those marks in terms of the physics and chemistry of the paper and ink."

There was a silence. And then his wife, seated beside him, said a bit too loudly, "Get out of that if you can."

However, to my amazement, he didn't try. He said, "John, for 40 years I've gone into my laboratory thinking that that could be done. But it can't."

In my astonishment at his honesty, I backtracked.

I said, "But science as we know it has only been going 500 years or so..."

He said, "It doesn't matter. You cannot explain the

semiotics bottom up solely in terms of the physics and chemistry of the paper and ink. You have to introduce an intelligent input to explain the semiotic dimension: the fact that the symbols carry meaning."

It then appeared to dawn on him that I wasn't bright enough to have thought of the argument. He said, "Where did you get that argument?"

I said, "I got it from a Nobel Prize winner."

I'm glad you laughed, ladies and gentlemen. It's interesting, isn't it, that given just a few marks on a page, we instantly argue upwards and postulate mind. And it is not a mind 'of the gaps' either.

But we are not quite finished. What about the human genome: 3.7 billion letters in a four letter chemical alphabet in exactly the right order like a computer program. Sophisticated, because the levels of information are contained not only in the linear sequencing of the DNA but in its folding and in its relationship to the cell. If we ask, as I do, about its ultimate origin we are told: "Chance and necessity."

What? "Chance and the laws of nature." We don't say that about a printed word even if it is only five letters long. What's the difference? Semiotics are involved in both cases.

It seems to me something very inconsistent is going on here. Text is evidence of mind, intelligence and information. What is more, we humans are not only containers of text in our DNA, we are producers of text, we can formulate thoughts in language. That, to my mind, is powerful evidence that naturalism is false. There is evidence of supernature already to be seen within you.

QUESTIONS FOR DISCUSSION

Christian faith is evidence-based, and Professor Lennox encourages us to follow the evidence wherever it leads. Where does the evidence he presented for the existence of God lead you?

What conclusions do you reach upon reflecting on Einstein's words: "The only incomprehensible thing about the universe is that it's comprehensible"?

To what extent do you believe you can trust your cognitive faculties? How does that belief affect your ability to search for truth?

Do you agree that the beginnings of supernature are already to be seen within you?

? For an audience question related to this topic (*How would a general belief in the supernatural change the way academic work is done?*) see page 33.

MIRACLES

POSSIBILITY OF MIRACLES

We come finally to the question of miracles. David Hume famously thought that miracles are, by definition, violations of natural laws and that natural laws are unalterably uniform. He deduced that miracles cannot occur. In light of that, Richard Dawkins has claimed that the nineteenth century was the last time when it was possible for an educated person to admit to believing in miracles.

It cannot be quite that simple because the aforementioned Nobel Prize winner, physicist William Phillips, believes that the resurrection of Jesus literally happened, as does physicist and Fellow of the Royal Society, Sir John Polkinghorne.

In order to focus this question, I'm going to concentrate on the central claim of Christianity: that Jesus Christ rose from the dead. Two issues are involved here. First of all, there is the question of the *a priori* possibility of miracle. Secondly, there is the question of the truth of any particular claim that a miracle has occurred – the resurrection of Jesus, for instance.

C.S. Lewis reminds us that the first fact of the history of Christendom is the number of people who say they've seen the resurrection. If they died without making anyone else believe this Gospel, no gospels would ever have been written.

Let's remind ourselves, then, of the contemporary scientific perspective. Since scientific laws embody cause and effect relationships, scientists nowadays do not regard them as merely capable of describing what has happened in the past (provided we're not working at the quantum level); such laws can successfully predict what'll happen in the future with such accuracy that even Newton's laws will land somebody on the moon. It is very natural, therefore, that such scientists resent the idea that some God could "arbitrarily intervene and alter, suspend, reverse or otherwise violate these laws of nature," to quote David Hume. To them, that would seem to contradict the immutability of the laws and thus overturn the very basis of the scientific understanding of the universe.

However, David Hume is guilty of inconsistency since he didn't believe in cause and effect, which is the foundation of the scientific laws just mentioned. And secondly, he thought, quite correctly, that you couldn't prove induction, which is also the foundation of many of our scientific laws.

Some time ago I had the opportunity to talk to philosopher Antony Flew, who as an atheist was the Richard Dawkins of a previous age. He was a world authority on David Hume. He told me: "I was wrong about Hume. All my books would have to be rewritten because Hume did not actually believe in cause and effect and his arguments against miracles fail." Unfortunately, Antony Flew did not live to do that work.

Objection: Only pre-scientific cultures believe in miracles. One argument is that belief in miracles in general and in the New Testament miracles in particular rose in a primitive, pre-scientific culture where people were ignorant of the laws of nature. That's sheer nonsense. A moment's thought shows us that in order for someone to recognize some event as a miracle, that person must know the corresponding regularity to which that event is an apparent exception. If you don't know that people who died normally stay in their graves, you would not recognize a resurrection as a miracle.

That principle was appreciated long ago. Joseph, for instance, who was espoused to Mary, knew exactly where babies came from. So when Mary said she was pregnant, Joseph as a God-fearing Jew wanted to divorce her. He wasn't ignorant of the laws of nature. His reason for later accepting Mary as his wife was that he became convinced that the child she was to bear was not conceived in immorality but, utterly uniquely, was conceived by the Holy Spirit.

It is simply false, therefore, to say that people did not know the laws of nature in those ancient days. In fact, there was a uniform attitude against resurrection. When the apostle Paul in his lecture to the philosophers at Athens mentioned Jesus rising from the dead (the word for resurrection is *anastasis*, Greek: to stand up again), they laughed. They would not have laughed if Paul had been simply asserting the survival of the soul, as that, for many of his audience, was a perfectly respectable view. They laughed because he was asserting something none of them believed in and that is the physical and bodily resurrection of a dead human being.

Objection: Nature is a closed system. The second objection is that now that we know the laws of nature, miracles are impossible, but that involves a further fallacy. Suppose I put $1,000 tonight in my hotel room in Cambridge and I put $1,000 in tomorrow night. One plus one equals two; that's $2,000. On the third day, I opened the drawer and I find $500. Now, what do I say? Do I say the laws of arithmetic have been broken? Or the laws of the United States have been broken?

Well, you obviously got the point. But see how important it is? First of all, you realize that a law of nature does not mean the same thing as a law of a country.

Secondly, when you only find $500 in the drawer, how do you know the laws of the United States have been broken? It's because you know the laws of arithmetic.

The laws of arithmetic have not been broken. What those laws tell you is that a thief has put his hand into the drawer and removed your cash. That is, something has come in from outside the system because it wasn't a closed system. This is crucial.

You see, as a scientist, I believe in the laws of nature.

Indeed, God, who is responsible for them, created an orderly universe; otherwise, as I said before, we'd never recognize an exception.

But God is not a prisoner of the laws of nature. They're not like the laws of the United States. God, who set the regularities there, can himself feed a new event into the system from outside. Science cannot stop Him doing that.

What Christians are claiming about the resurrection of Jesus is not that he rose by some natural processes; that would violate the laws of nature. No. Christians claim that Jesus rose because God injected enormous power and energy from outside the system. Now, unless you have evidence that the system is totally closed, you cannot argue against the possibility of miracles.

QUESTIONS FOR DISCUSSION

Professor Lennox quotes Dawkins saying that the nineteenth century is the last time when it was possible for the educated person to admit to believing in miracles. Did you find Professor Lennox's rebuttal convincing?

Do you believe we live in a closed system? Why is it important to distinguish between violating the laws of a closed system and working from outside a potentially open system?

MIRACLES

ACTUALITY OF MIRACLES

So, now you have to come to the actuality of miracles. Is there evidence anywhere that a miracle has occurred? Christianity is based on the claim that there is evidence Jesus Christ came alive from the dead. How do you approach the matter of evidence when the event to which you are referring is a unique singularity that seems highly improbable?

After all, if you were to take people from Harvard and set them in graveyards to watch for a month and write in their books whether they saw a resurrection or not, you could scientifically show by statistical methods that resurrections are very improbable in the Harvard area. But unless you've investigated every grave back to the beginning of the universe, you cannot say a resurrection is impossible.

But the question is: Is there actual evidence that the resurrection of Jesus happened?

What are the facts? There is an empty tomb.

How do we know? To answer that we need to investigate the historical evidence, a task for which I would need at least another lecture.

Since I cannot do that today let me tell you what I have done. I have read through David Hume paying particular attention to his criteria for evidence and his views on the credibility of witnesses. I then considered the evidence for the resurrection of Jesus from this perspective and, if you will forgive another shameless bit of advertising, I've just produced a book that contains my arguments. The book is called *Gunning for God*.

My final point is this. Science and history are not the only sources of evidence for the existence of God, miracle and the supernatural. Personal experience is enormously important even to a professor who's interested in intellectual things, because one of the prime evidences, to me, that the Christian faith is true is my personal experience over many years of the living reality of Christ in my life. If He's risen from the dead, it follows that He's alive and that opens up the possibility of having a relationship with Him. So, that too, would be a very important thing to explore.

I started by reminding you of Harvard's motto: *Veritas*. But that is not what it used to be. I was delighted to see the original motto still adorning one of your main buildings: *Veritas Christo et Ecclesiae*. Truth for Christ and the Church. I would suggest to you, Harvard students and professors, the time has come to revisit that original meaning.

MIRACLES

QUESTIONS FOR DISCUSSION

Professor Lennox refers to experiencing the living reality of Christ in his life. What weight do you place on personal experience in forming your beliefs about the supernatural? Can you pinpoint pivotal moments shaping those beliefs?

? Christianity is based on the improbable claim that Jesus Christ came alive from the dead. Professor Lennox discusses the implications of this claim in a question from the audience, saying that because Christ died and rose, he "is the only person that offers me the knowledge of forgiveness right here and now in this life based not on my merit but on my trust in him and his merit." For more about how the resurrection differentiates Christianity and the implications of this belief, see page 44.

? For more audience questions related to this topic, see page 39 (*If I were to tell you I was just resurrected from the dead, what evidence would you require to believe it?*) and page 40 (*Do you believe that there are examples of God's supernatural intervention today and have there been any in your life?*).

QUESTION AND ANSWER

MIRACLES

Summary of Questions from the Moderator

- Could you tell us a little bit more about what got you interested in these questions of the supernatural, God and the relation to science? (Answer on page 31)

- How would a general belief in the supernatural change the way academic work is done? And should that happen? (Answer on page 33)

- Should we look at these questions with regard to the miraculous using the methods of science or should this be left to theologians and to philosophers? (Answer on page 35)

Summary of Questions from the Audience

- How do you approach people who don't care? Who neither believe nor do not believe? (Answer on page 38)

- If I were to tell you I was just resurrected from the dead, what evidence would you require to believe it? (Answer on page 39)

- Do you believe that there are examples of God's supernatural intervention today and have there been any in your life? (Answer on page 40)

- You claim that science and religion do not make exclusive truth claims. Various world religions, however, do make exclusive truth claims. How can we know that Christianity is right at the exclusion of others? (Answer on page 44)

Question and Answer Session

Moderator: First, could you tell us a little bit more about what got you interested in these questions of the supernatural, God and the relation to science?

Lennox: Well, as I said, I come from Ireland, which has a pretty poor reputation for religion, yet I was very fortunate to have parents who were Christian and not sectarian and who loved me enough to allow me to think. And what I mean by that is this. I remember my father saying to me when I was about 13, "Have you ever read Marx?" And I said, "No." "Well," he said, "I think you'd better." And he handed me *The Communist Manifesto.*

He was not an educated man. He'd love to have had the education he enabled me to have. I was the first in my family to get to university and was very fortunate to get the opportunity to go to Cambridge.

But the habits of thought and open enquiry in our home lived with me when I got to university. Now, when, as I mentioned in my talk, the student challenged me about my Irishness and said, "Of course you believe in God; it's all Irish genetics," I'd heard that many times, but it occurred to me that I now was being given a real opportunity at Cambridge to get to know students who did not share my worldview. That was the first of many experiences that prepared me, for example, to face Peter Singer.

He said, as I mentioned, that his big objection to religion is that people end up where they started – believing what their parents did. Well, Singer doesn't seem to have a lot of experience with people changing their worldview. My experience at Cambridge in

England was that people who started from non-religious presuppositions, from atheism or agnosticism, could, as a result of considering the evidence, come to faith in Christ and have their lives transformed. Seeing that happen was a very powerful bit of evidence for me, because I personally do not know what it is like to be an adult and not believe in God.

That early encounter at university set me on a path that eventually led to my going to Eastern Europe where I met (in East Germany particularly) many people who'd been systematically exposed to atheistic philosophy in their schools and education. Subsequently I had many opportunities to go to Russia. Indeed, I have spent a great deal of my life exposing my faith to its opposite.

Why? Because I'm actually interested in *veritas*, in getting to know the truth. I'm not interested in religion that is simply a comfort prop, a wish fulfillment *a la* Sigmund Freud. I want to know the truth.

Moderator: How does some of what you were saying about the possibility of the supernatural relate to our day-to-day work as academics? A lot of academic work proceeds under what might be called an assumption of methodological naturalism: even if we believe in the supernatural, we often set those beliefs aside for the purposes of academic study and research. That supposedly leads to more common ground and a common method for study, and allows for consensus amongst those with very different beliefs. So, how would a general belief in the supernatural change the way academic work is done? And should that happen?

Lennox: I don't find the term methodological naturalism particularly helpful. It seems to me for 99 percent of science, it makes no difference whether you think the universe is apparently designed or actually designed. So, methodological theism would work as well as methodological naturalism.

The problem comes here with what I would call the truth quest. Could it be that there are times where philosophical presuppositions affect the science? Now, in 99 percent of cases, they don't because scientists are studying how some bit of nature works. For instance, what are the equations governing this diffusion? What are the statistics of the latest epidemic? They are not concerned with questions of ultimate origin or significance here so the God question does not arise.

However, there is an important question to be asked: could it be that studying a system under naturalistic presupposition raises questions that are insolvable at that level so that we must look outside naturalism to a higher level of the input of mind? That's where the real problem comes.

Richard Lewontin, a very distinguished geneticist, said something like: "Science doesn't force us into methodological naturalism. It is our *a priori* conviction of naturalism that forces us to look for a purely naturalistic solution...however counter-intuitive, we must not let a divine foot enter the door."

This is a very honest admission that it is not science but an *a priori* naturalism that determines what in the end is to be believed as science.

When we're studying the question of genetic information, for instance, it is perfectly legitimate to attempt to account for its origin naturalistically. However, I would suggest our lack of progress may well be the result of failing to open our minds to following the evidence (rather than the naturalistic prejudice) and entertaining the idea that mind may be involved.

Antony Flew, who I mentioned before, was a prominent atheist who converted to Deism late in life and he was asked how this happened. His answer was that he saw in DNA the evidence of intelligent input.

I want to be free to follow the evidence where it leads. That is, to my mind, the true Socratic spirit of science. To force a naturalistic paradigm on everything has the effect of closing down science rather than opening it up.

Moderator: So, following up that, I'm wondering to what extent is the miraculous open to scientific inquiry and scientific methods. Within medicine and public health, believe it or not, there are randomized trials to look at whether prayer is effective or not. And some of these studies have found an effect. Others have not. And there have been meta-analysis made looking at this question. One published in a prestigious medical journal suggested there was an effect. Another one published by a very reputable group that focuses on meta-analysis suggested that there wasn't.

Is this sort of thing reasonable to do? Should we look at these questions with regard to the miraculous using the methods of science or should this be left to theologians and to philosophers?

Lennox: Well, I'll have to give a short answer. I think we should apply the methodology appropriate to the claim and if the claim is that a certain thing happened – let's take the resurrection – as a fact of history, what are the appropriate methods? Well, of course the resurrection is a singularity and it's highly improbable and it leads us into a realm of science that often is not carefully defined enough. What I mean by that is this: normally, when we think of science, we think of inductive methods. We do an experiment 100 times. We get the same result and we expect that to happen the 101st time.

Well, you can't repeat a resurrection to see if it happened or not and what we therefore have to employ are the methods of forensic science. The body of John Lennox lies on the floor, he's dead. You can't say, "Well, let's rerun the experiment to see what happened."

But you can get at the truth of what happened by methods that are often called historical science. I would certainly call them that because they – natural sciences – have got those two branches: inductive science and historical science. Historical science is important and mainstream: the whole history of the universe only happened once and cosmologists are constantly investigating singularities by these kinds of methods.

Now, because miracles are *a priori* highly improbable, Francis Collins (the Director of the National Institute of Health, as you probably know, was an atheist, became a Christian) gives an important bit of cautionary advice. He says that we mustn't rush into accepting claims to the miraculous since there are a lot of fraudulent claims. I agree with him very much. But he, like myself, believes that the resurrection passes the evidence test with flying colors.

Now, to come directly to your question of meta-analyses. I have been reading a book by a former president of the Royal College of Psychiatrists in the UK, Professor Andrew Sims, in which he responds to Dawkins' notion that religion has zero benefits. Sims says that the vast volume of academic literature shows that religious belief has a beneficial effect. And he adds that if the findings had gone in the opposite direction and it had been found that religious belief is bad for you, it would have been front-page news in every newspaper in the world. The fact that the correlation is positive, that belief in God is good for you, is one of "psychiatry's best kept secrets."

I am, however, highly skeptical though, about experiments of the sort that gets one group praying for one man and another group not praying for another man, and seeing what happens.

I'm very skeptical of the results because the experiment makes nonsense of what is meant by real prayer. What I'm not skeptical of is my own experience of answers to prayer and guidance in life.

Lennox: I'll now have a go at the questions from the audience. You're about to experience the limits of my ignorance. Because this is a Q&A, ladies and gentlemen, all I can do is to suggest my approach to these questions for you to think about.

Let's have a look at the first one. How do I approach people who don't care, who neither believe nor do not believe?

I try to care for them. If people don't care, there's usually a reason and it often is a very complex, psychological reason. I'm very fortunate to have two loving parents. Some people have none. And the idea of a God who loves them is very hard to grasp. It means nothing to them.

It seems to me that people who don't care are saying something about themselves that goes very deep and I would like to find out a little bit more of why they don't care, provided I don't intrude too far into their private space. I believe that God is extremely interested in people who don't care, because they often have very good reasons for not caring.

I was taught very early on that every person is of infinite value. I really do believe that every one of you is of infinite value, made in the image of God as Genesis says. You're more important than the sun. You know it's there; it doesn't know you're there. You realize that, don't you?

If there is a God who cares for you and you don't care about him, there's a disjoint somewhere. I would want to try very gently to find out exactly what's going on. It may be you don't care because you have had a very negative experience of religion, of Christian religion, alas, sometimes.

Lennox: Now, second question, if you were to tell me that you were just resurrected, what evidence would I require to believe it?

Well, I would want evidence that you died. But I'd want more. I'd want evidence that you were buried. And actually, that raises a very interesting question because when we come to study historiographically the resurrection of Jesus, the fact that he died (and it's historically attested) and was buried (and it's historically attested) is part of the evidence. So, when you show me you've died, then I'll take your claim seriously.

Lennox: Now, are there examples of God's intervention today and in my own life?

That's a very personal question and there's always the danger in attempting to answer this of rationalization. What will convince one person will not convince another. I believe in the resurrection because I think we have got more than enough evidence at the objective, historical level. History's never completely objective, of course, but as contrasted with the evidence of my subjective experience.

You ask about my life. I have a wife. We've been married 43 years. I've got three children and I've got five grandchildren. We pray together. We discuss scripture together. I couldn't begin to enumerate to you the times when things have happened in life that you could attribute to coincidence, if you wish, but where my experience on the inside tells me that coincidence is totally inadequate. Would you like me to tell you about one of them?

I very rarely do this, but here goes.

As you know, I have been a lot to Russia. How did I come to go to Russia? Well, I'll tell you. I was at a conference of mathematical cryptographers. You all depend on them when it comes to the security of your money in the bank.

The conference was in Belgium and after it was over the bus driver took a detour to the station with the result that we missed the train. So, there were 50 irritable mathematicians standing on the platform in Belgium. I was going to Cologne in Germany and it was late at night. I was a bit concerned. I had a heavy suitcase and in those days, Cologne station wasn't the best place to be found after midnight.

When the train arrived, I found myself in a compartment with a German, a Belgian and two Russians. I sat beside one of the Russians and I started to talk to him. He was rather surprised that I could speak a bit of his language.

"What do you do?"

He said, "I'm an ecologist."

"Oh," I said, "Ecologist? Do they have those in Russia?"

And he said, "Yes, and this is the first time I've been out in the west. I come from Lake Baikal."

So I said, "Can you openly talk about ecology in Russia?"

He said, "Well, you know, we can say a bit."

And then I said to him, "Are there other things that you can talk about openly that were taboo earlier?"

He said, "Like what?"

I said, "Like God, for example."

And he said, "Yes, we can talk about God."

In that moment, a thought rushed into my mind, "I've got to give this man a Bible. But this is crazy. I mean, where do you get a Bible from in the middle of the night on a train going through Belgium? "

Then I remembered. Three weeks before that, I'd been in Germany with a publisher friend. Sitting on his desk was a Russian Bible. He said, "Would you like to have it? I can't read it." I said, "I'd love it. Mine is pretty old and I'd like that." So, I put it in my suitcase. The question that now arose in the train was: was the Bible still there?

While I kept talking to the Russian man, I got up, put my hand into the suitcase and found the Bible. I took it out and I handed it to him saying, "That is for you". He went as white as a sheet. He couldn't speak and I thought he had taken ill.

I said, "What's wrong?"

He said, "How did you know?"

I said, "What do you mean, how did I know?"

He said, "How did you know that six weeks ago, the only Bible we've ever seen was stolen from our home in Siberia? This is our first visit to the West and in four hours' time we're taking the plane to Moscow. So, how did you know?"

I said, "Do you believe there's a God?"

He said, "I don't know, but," he said, "look in the corner. That's my wife. She believes."

And I turned – I'll never forget it – to see this young woman with her face glowing, the tears streaming down her face as she clutched the Bible and she said, "Is that really for me? Are you really giving it to me?"

I said, "Of course." A few moments later the train stopped at their station and they were gone in the night.

The German student said to me, "Does that often happen to you?"

I said, "No, it doesn't. But you shouldn't think it strange."

She said, "Why not?"

"Well," I said, "Look. This person comes from a country where they've been systematically denied access to the Bible. If this really is the word of God, surely God can use me as a postman?"

"Well then," she said, "I better read it." So she did – but that is another story.

When I arrived home I told my wife what had happened. She

then did something she's never done in her life before or since. She said, "You will need to clear your schedule for at least two months."

I said, "Pardon?"

She said, "You're going to Russia."

I said, "Why?"

She said, "How would you go to Russia?"

"Well," I said, "it's a very complicated business. You've got to ring the Royal Society, fill in endless forms and so on."

She said, "Ring them."

"Well," I said, "perhaps next week."

"Right now."

Something told me she was right. I phoned and the official who replied said: "Dr Lennox, you want to go to Russia? When can you go? How long can you go for? You see we want the Russian mathematicians to visit our country now that the possibility is open. The problem is that our agreement is that if we want one of their scientists for a month we have to find a British scientist prepared to go to Russia for the same length of time and very few are prepared to go. Can you go for a month?"

I said, "My wife says two."

He said, "Done. No forms. You will get the money; you can leave tomorrow if you want."

When I got to Russia as a visitor to the Academy of Sciences I found to my astonishment that their main interest was in how could a person like me believe in God. I can't tell you what flowed from that, but I firmly believe it was an intervention God.

I expect such things to happen all the time because God is real.

Lennox: The last question is about the fact that there are different religions, so why would one be a Christian and not something else?

So how do I approach this question? Well, in exactly the same way as everything else: it is a matter of assembling the evidence. Let's take the three great monotheistic religions. They hold different views about the resurrection of Jesus. My Jewish friends believe that Jesus died and did not rise. My Muslim friends believe he didn't die. I believe the he both died and rose. These three views cannot all be true. So how do you approach a question like that?

The first point to make is that as you go around the world and study people of all religions or none you'll find the striking fact that there's a common element of morality that's shared by almost every living human being. For instance, the golden rule – "Do unto others as you would be done by" – is to be found in every single religion, in every philosophy from Roman paganism to British humanism. What does that tell me?

It tells me that we share a common humanity and a common morality and so we need to respect each other's moral integrity. Sometimes, as a Christian, I can be put to shame by the moral integrity of someone of another religion or an atheist. My experience is that if we recognize the moral integrity of others we can much more easily discuss the differences that exist.

The next point is that these differences come not at the level of ethics and morality so much as at the level of the basis on which a person can have a relationship with God. Broadly speaking, there are two views.

One of the views likens religion to what you experience at Harvard University. There is an entrance examination to be faced at the beginning. We can imagine that as a door here. And then this wavy line that follows the door represents our time of study when we listen to the professors who teach us and try to merit good assessments. At the end there is a great gate to be faced. It's called Final Exams. Now, the whole principle on which the system depends is that of merit. The professors, all of them, are very kind, I'm sure, but they cannot guarantee that you're going to get through the door at the end, can they? It depends on your merit. Your performance. Your achievement.

Many religions are like that as their adherents will tell you. There's an initiation rite at the beginning through which you get on the way. You then try to follow the way, the teachings, ritual etc. and you hope that when the great final assessment comes and your good deeds are measured against your bad deeds that somehow the good ones will weigh more than the bad ones and you will be accepted into whatever is beyond.

That is what many people believe. That is what religion is. A system of merit whereby we gain God's acceptance. In that sense, Christianity is not a religion. The unique thing about Christianity is that it teaches that salvation and acceptance by God are not based on merit. Because it does have a gate, in a way, but at the beginning there stands Jesus Christ who claims to have come into the world to die for my sin. Now, that's a very ugly word to raise at Harvard, but you did ask me about religions, so I'll have to give you the answer that I believe is the truth.

In other words, let me put it this way. My first day at Cambridge,

I saw a beautiful girl. I married her eventually. Suppose I had gone to her and said, "Sally, you know, I'd like to marry you, but here's a cookbook. It's got a whole lot of rules inside it. Now, if you keep those rules fairly well for the next 30 or 40 years, I will think about accepting you. Of course, I couldn't possibly accept you now, but if you perform well enough, when the final assessment comes, I will accept you."

But you see, that would have been to insult her.

The secret of my marriage, ladies and gentlemen, is this: that we accepted each other at the beginning. Unconditionally. And because she doesn't have to keep the rules in the cookbook, so to speak, in order to gain my acceptance, that sets her free to learn to cook. And it's exactly the same with God. We wouldn't dream of basing a relationship with a fellow human being on a measured performance and an acceptance at the end of a long history of performing laws, and yet millions of people think that that's the way to base a relationship with God.

Christianity competes with no other religion here for the simple reason that Christ is the only person that offers me the knowledge of forgiveness right here and now. This is possible because his salvation and acceptance are not based on my merit – not on what I have done but on the merit of Jesus Christ who died and rose for me. I therefore try to live for him not in order to gain his acceptance but because, ladies and gentlemen, I already have it.

QUESTIONS FOR DISCUSSION

From *Origins* **(page 4)**

- Do you have close friends, as Professor Lennox does, who do not share your worldview? How do you engage them in conversation about those worldviews?

- What do you think the general climate on campus is? Is belief in God an insult to the intellect? Why?

From *The Real Conflict: Worldviews* **(page 6)**

- Does shifting the conflict from science/religion to naturalism/theism make a difference?

- Which way does your worldview tend: naturalism or theism? How would your understanding of reality be different if you adopted the opposite worldview from the one you hold?

- If you find yourself an intellectual theist but practical naturalist, or vice versa, how could you align your beliefs and practice to be consistent?

From *The First Confusion: Nature of Faith* **(page 11)**

- Do you agree that scientism is the reigning view? Can you think of examples you've seen, heard or read recently?

- If "rationality is bigger than science," as Professor Lennox argues, what are other ways to find truth?

- Do you find the debunking of any of these "myths" surprising? Compelling? Questionable?

From *The Second Confusion: Nature of Explanation* **(page 14)**

- Professor Lennox says that he does not believe in a "God of the gaps" but rather, "God of the whole show." In the Q&A he refers to a "God who is extremely interested in people who don't care" (see page 38). What is your view of who God is (or is not)? How did you come to this view?

From *The Role of Faith in Science* **(page 21)**

- Christian faith is evidence-based, and Professor Lennox encourages us to follow the evidence wherever it leads. Where does the evidence he presented for the existence of God lead you?

- What conclusions do you reach upon reflecting on Einstein's words: "The only incomprehensible thing about the universe is that it's comprehensible"?

- To what extent do you believe you can trust your cognitive faculties? How does that belief affect your ability to search for truth?

- Do you agree that the beginnings of supernature are already to be seen within you?

From *Possibility of Miracles* **(page 25)**

- Professor Lennox quotes Dawkins saying that the nineteenth century is the last time when it was possible for the educated person to admit to believing in miracles. Did you find Professor Lennox's rebuttal convincing?

- Do you believe we live in a closed system? Why is it important to distinguish between violating the laws of a closed system and working from outside a potentially open system?

From *Actuality of Miracles* **(page 28)**

- Professor Lennox refers to experiencing the living reality of Christ in his life. What weight do you place on personal experience in forming your beliefs about the supernatural? Can you pinpoint pivotal moments shaping your beliefs?

ABOUT THE VERITAS FORUM

The Veritas Forum hosts university events that engage students and faculty in discussions about life's hardest questions and the relevance of Jesus Christ to all of life.

Every year, hundreds of university community members host, plan and coordinate a Veritas Forum on their local campuses, with guidance from national and regional staff across North America and Europe.

We seek to inspire the shapers of tomorrow's culture to connect their hardest questions with the person and story of Jesus Christ.

For more information about The Veritas Forum, including recordings and upcoming events, visit www.veritas.org.

Printed in Great Britain
by Amazon